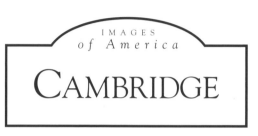

IMAGES
of America

CAMBRIDGE

D1277148

The Soldiers' Monument on Cambridge Common pays tribute to the 939 men from Cambridge who gave the ultimate sacrifice during the Civil War. The cornerstone was laid on June 17, 1869, and the completed monument was solemnly dedicated by veterans and residents on July 13, 1870. The 30-foot square base has bas-reliefs representing the four arms of service—navy, cavalry, artillery, and infantry; a statue of a soldier at ease surmounts the 55-foot, 8-inch-tall monument.

In Memory of Stephen Davies Paine (1932-1997)

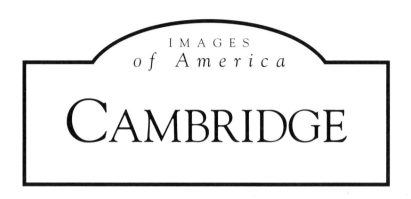

IMAGES
of America

CAMBRIDGE

ADAMS STREET

Anthony Mitchell Sammarco

ARCADIA

Published by Arcadia Publishing,
an imprint of Tempus Publishing, Inc.
2 Cumberland Street
Charleston, SC 29401

Printed in Great Britain.

Library of Congress Catalog Card Number: Applied for.

For all general information contact Arcadia Publishing at:
Telephone 843-853-2070
Fax 843-853-0044
E-Mail arcadia@charleston.net

For customer service and orders:
Toll-Free 1-888-313-BOOK

Visit us on the internet at http://www.arcadiaimages.com

A group photograph of early editors of the *Harvard Lampoon* shows, from left to right, the following: (standing) Barrett T. Wendell (1877), F.J. Stimson (1876), R. Grant (1873), W.S. Otis (1878); (seated) Charles A. Coolidge (1881), J.P. Bowen (1879), John T. Wheelwright (1876), Jefferson T. Coolidge (1879), F.P. Attwood (1878), and F. McLennan (1879).

4

CONTENTS

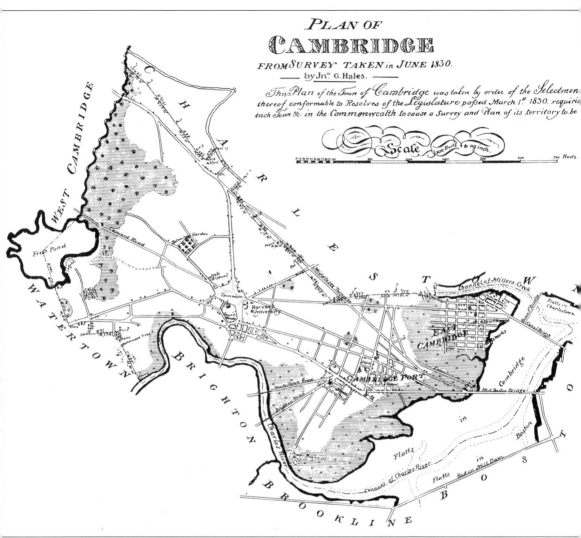

A "Plan of Cambridge from the Survey Taken in June 1830 by John G. Hales" shows Cambridge with Harvard Square in the center, East Cambridge and Cambridgeport on the right, and Fresh Pond and North Cambridge on the left.

INTRODUCTION

Settled in 1631, Cambridge was originally known as New Towne and was referred to by William Wood, an English chronicler of early 17th-century aspects of New England, as "one of the neatest and best-compacted towns in New England, having many fair structures, with many handsome-contrived streets. The inhabitants are most of them very rich." The town was laid out in squares with the early streets, such as Creek, Marsh, Long, Crooked, Wood, Spring, and Water Streets, laid out at right angles, one square remaining open as the marketplace. In 1631, a passage was dug connecting the Charles River and South Street, the first of subsequent topographical changes. Although New Towne had been envisioned as the seat of government for the Massachusetts Bay Colony, the focus eventually shifted to Boston. However, the early years of the town were important, as was evidenced by the founding in 1636 of Harvard College with 400 pounds appropriated by the general court. Endowed in 1638 with one half of the estate and the entire library of the Rev. John Harvard (1607–1638) of Charlestown, this fledgling school was to be the first college founded in the New World. It was said that "in compliment to the college, and in memory of the place where many of our fathers received their education, [the town] was now denominated *Cambridge*"; and so it has been known since.

Although Cambridge was closely associated with Harvard College for the first two centuries after the town was settled, the area known as Old Cambridge was the center of town and is today the area known as Harvard Square. Considered no more than a farming village until the beginning of the 19th century, Cambridge was to attract new residents, immigrants to the New World, and thereby an individuality and a sense of urbanity which separated it from Boston. The town was to see the increased development of Cambridgeport and East Cambridge, two areas that began to flourish as residential areas in the early 19th century, with manufacturing and businesses attracting these new residents. Although Cambridge had open farmland that was well cultivated, the town was known for its fisheries along the Alewife and Charles Rivers and the various industries that brought it great renown.

During the early 19th century, the aspect of arboretum cemeteries had been introduced to this country by those who had visited Pere La Chaise in Paris. In 1831, Sweet Auburn, a large tract of land with gently rolling hills and valleys on the Cambridge-Watertown line, was purchased and laid out as Mount Auburn Cemetery. Dedicated on September 24, 1831, Mount Auburn was laid out by Henry A.S. Dearborn with winding paths embellished with infinite varieties of tree and shrub. The sale of family lots went briskly and secured the success of Mount Auburn. Although this large tract of land was to be used as a "garden for the dead," Cambridge's rapid development ensured its incorporation as a city, which was accomplished in 1846.

On May 4, 1846, the first city government of Cambridge assembled in the church at the corner of Norfolk and Harvard Streets and began to transact business on behalf of the city. The first mayor of Cambridge was the Rev. James D. Green who, with the support of the city council, began the mechanics of creating a city with ordinances to regulate the "racing and immoderate driving of horses in the streets, keeping of swine, transporting of gunpowder, and the 'going at large' of domestic fowl and goats" (the travails of city government!). By the mid-19th century, Cambridge had become a city of thriving enterprises, successful businesses, and well-kept houses. Transportation had increased with horse-drawn streetcars connecting Cambridge and Boston and was to be greatly improved in the early 20th century with the opening of the Cambridge subway, which connected Harvard Square and Boston. The industrial base included books and printing (the first book to be published in the New World was *The Bay Psalm Book*, written by Thomas Weld, Richard Mather, and John Eliot, and published in Cambridge in 1640 by Stephen Daye), bricks, confectionery, soap, furniture, tinware, glassware, musical instruments, and metal goods— all of which provided employment for the burgeoning population. The great strides made in the period between the Civil War and World War II established Cambridge as not only an attractive and convenient place for people of all walks of life and ethnic traditions to live, but also a city known throughout the country for its rich historical associations.

> *Home of culture and wide learning,*
> *Generous to all;*
> *Knowledge, letters, names renowned*
> *Answer to her call;*
> *To the world she's given all freely.*
> *Cambridge, honored be,*
> *City fair, with gifts most rare,*
> *Praise to thee!*
>
> —Downs

One

EARLY CAMBRIDGE

Know old Cambridge? Hope you do.
Born there? Don't say so? I was, too;
Born in a house with a gambrel-roof,
Standing still, if you must have proof.
—Holmes

Christ Church was designed by Peter Harrison and stands at Zero Garden Street, opposite the Cambridge Common. During the Revolution, as most of its congregation were Loyalists, the church was closed and used as a barracks by Connecticut troops; the organ pipes were melted down for bullets to supply the colonists. The burying ground adjacent to the church is the oldest in Cambridge, having been paled in 1635 and used as both a sheep pasture and a graveyard until 1702.

The Cooper-Frost-Austin House was built c. 1690 by Deacon Jonathan Cooper and is today among the oldest houses in Cambridge. Standing at 21 Linnaean Street, which was laid out in 1724, the house was acquired by the Society for the Preservation of New England Antiquities in 1912.

Edward Holyoke (1689–1769) was president of Harvard College from 1737 until his death. Holyoke Street was named in his honor.

The Brattle House was built
c. 1740 and stands at 42 Brattle
Street; this was the residence of
Brig. Gen. William Brattle. As
Brattle was a Loyalist, the house
was used as headquarters by Col.
Thomas Mifflin, quartermaster to
the Continental army during the
Revolution. Today, the house is the
headquarters of the Cambridge
Center for Adult Education.

William Brattle (1702–1776)
was a noted preacher, lawyer, and
physician. Since he was a Loyalist,
Brattle left Boston for Halifax, Nova
Scotia, in 1776 with the British
troops.

The Washington Elm shields the house of Deacon Josiah Moore, which stood on the present site of the Shepard Memorial Church. An assessor, overseer of the poor, and selectman, Deacon Moore purchased the house in 1784. On the right can be seen the granite and rail fence which surrounded the Cambridge Common.

In 1886, the Washington Elm was photographed with its cast-iron fence enclosure and tablet commemorating its importance to the events of the Revolution. It was under the arching branches of this tree on July 3, 1775, that Gen. George Washington took command of the Continental army.

A goodly elm of noble girth
That thrice the human span
While on their variegated course
The constant seasons ran
Through gale and hail and fiery bolt
Has stood erect as man.

The birthplace of Oliver Wendell Holmes (1809–1894) was a Colonial gambrel-roofed house built in 1737 on land between Kirkland Street and Massachusetts Avenue. It was here that Holmes wrote the stirring lines to *Old Ironsides*, which effectively saved the U.S.S. *Constitution* from an ignoble end. Austin Hall, designed by H.H. Richardson for the Harvard Law School, was built in 1881 behind the Holmes House, which survived until 1884.

The Wadsworth House was built in 1726 by the Rev. Benjamin Wadsworth (1669–1737), president of Harvard College from 1725 to 1736. It remained as the president's house of Harvard College until the presidency of Jared Sparks (1849–1853). During the Revolution, the house served successively as the headquarters of Gen. George Washington and Maj. Gen. Charles Lee. On the right can be seen Boylston Hall, designed by Schultze and Schoen and built in 1857.

The Hooper-Lee-Nichols House was built in the 1680s and remodeled c. 1760. It stands at 159 Brattle Street, near Appleton Street. Here lived Judge Joseph Lee, who is credited with adding its third floor. The roof balustrade is made from mahogany balusters that were once part of the communion rail of Saint Paul's Church in Boston. Today, this is the headquarters of the Cambridge Historical Society.

The Ruggles House was built c. 1764 by the Jamaican planter George Ruggles and later became the home of Thomas Fayerweather. Located at 175 Brattle Street, it is an impressive three-story mansion along "Tory Row," as Brattle Street is often referred to.

The Vassall House at the corner of Brattle and Hawthorne Streets was a 17th-century house that was remodeled c. 1746. Here lived Henry Vassall and his wife, Penelope Royall, daughter of the wealthy merchant Isaac Royall of Medford. During the Revolution, the house served as the medical headquarters of the American army, as well as the residence and prison of Dr. Benjamin Church.

The Lechmere House was built in 1761 on Brattle Street by Richard Lechmere, a distiller for whom Lechmere Square was named. The house is also known as the Riedesel House, after Baron von Riedesel who was imprisoned here during the Revolution. During the winter of 1778–79, after the surrender of Burgoyne's army, Riedesel, a Hessian officer in that army, was held here with his wife. Riedesel Avenue, on the side of the property, was named for him. The house was later remodeled by John Brewster, who raised it and added a new first floor.

The Read House originally stood at the corner of Brattle Street and Farwell Place. Built *c.* 1772 by the patriot James Read, it was a quaint house set in a large garden. The property was sold by the Read Family in 1826 to Levi Farwell, treasurer of Harvard College, for whom the side street was named.

The Inman House was built by Ralph Inman (1726–1788) on a large estate bounded by Massachusetts Avenue, Harvard, Inman, and Austin Streets in Cambridgeport. The commodious three-story house was noted for the hospitality that was dispensed there prior to the Revolution. In 1775, the Inman House was the headquarters of General Putnam. The house was moved in 1873 to the corner of Brookline and Auburn Streets, and the original site was subdivided for house lots.

Christ Church was designed by Peter Harrison, who is considered the first architect in America. The church was built in 1760 on Garden Street, opposite the Cambridge Common. The first minister of the church was the Rev. East Apthorp. During the Revolution, Gen. George Washington worshiped here. A chime of 13 bells, known as the Harvard Chime, was presented to Christ Church by the alumni of Harvard College in 1860.

The interior of Christ Church is an elegant space with monumental Ionic columns supporting a heavily dentiled cornice. Interestingly, there is no gallery and the original proportions were altered in 1857 when the church was lengthened by two bays.

The Apthorp House was built in 1760 by the Rev. East Apthorp, first minister of Christ Church. Located at 10 Linden Street, the house was often referred to as the Bishop's Palace, in reference to the grandeur of the Anglican church. The house was used as the headquarters of General Putnam during the Battle of Bunker Hill.

The Waterhouse House was built c. 1753 by Dr. Benjamin Waterhouse at what is now 7 Waterhouse Street. A noted physician, scientist and Harvard professor, Waterhouse is credited with having introduced vaccination to this country, inoculating his own children against smallpox to reassure the public of its ultimate benefits.

The Fuller House was built in 1807 at 71 Cherry Street, near Central Square. Here lived the Fuller family, of whom Sarah Margaret Fuller, later the Marchesa d'Ossoli, was born. In 1902, the house became a settlement house and has been used as such ever since.

Timothy Fuller (1778–1835) was the Middlesex County attorney from 1811 to 1813. Considered a man of exceptional ability as a lawyer and statesman, he served in Congress from 1817 to 1825.

The Fay House was designed by Charles Bulfinch (1763–1844) and built in 1806 for Nathaniel Ireland, a maker of ironwork for ships. The house was later the home of Judge Samuel Fay, whose daughter called the house "Castle Corners" and sold it in 1885 to Radcliffe College. The house was enlarged in 1890 by the noted architectural firm of Longfellow, Alden, and Harlow.

Samuel Phillips Prescott Fay (1766–1856) was judge of probate court in Middlesex County from 1821 to 1856.

The Dana House was built *c.* 1822 by Chief Justice Dana. The house was purchased by Harvard College in 1835, and a cupola with a revolving dome was added to its roof. This addition served as the first observatory for the college. In 1947, the house was moved across Quincy Street and the Lamont Library was built on the original site.

Iroquois Indians pose in full regalia on the stops of the Craigie-Longfellow House in 1910. Their visit to the former home of the great writer Henry Wadsworth Longfellow proved to be both an interesting and a uniquely colorful one.

The Craigie-Longfellow House was built in 1759 by the Jamaican planter Col. John Vassall Jr. A Loyalist, Vassel became a fugitive under British protection during the siege and the house was used by Gen. George Washington as his headquarters for eight months. In 1791, Andrew Craigie purchased the estate, after which it was sold by his widow in 1843 to Henry Wadsworth Longfellow. Today, the house is preserved by the Longfellow Memorial Association and is open to the public.

Henry Wadsworth Longfellow (1807–1882) on the right, and his friend U.S. Sen. Charles Sumner (1811–1874), a noted abolitionist, were photographed around the late 1860s.
With reference to his house, Longfellow wrote a poem about Gen. George Washington:

Once, ah, once within these walls,
One whom memory oft recalls,
The Father of his Country dwelt.
And yonder meadows broad and damp
The fires of the besieging camp,
Encircled with a burning belt.
Up and down these echoing stairs,
Heavy with the weight of cares,
Sounded his majestic tread; Yes,
within this very room
Sat he in those hours of gloom,
Weary both in heart and head.
—Longfellow

Longfellow's study contained many books and objets d'art, including portraits of Ralph Waldo Emerson, of Nathaniel Hawthorne, and of himself, displayed on the easel in the center of this photograph. In this room, surrounded by his friends' portraits, he wrote *Tales of the Wayside Inn*, *The Courtship of Myles Standish*, and *The Song of Hiawatha*. Notice the gas pipe descending from the gasolier to illuminate the center table lamp, where he often read and wrote.

The stair hall in the Craigie-Longfellow House has fine Colonial paneling and a grandfather clock on the stair landing.

LOWELL HOUSE

The Oliver-Lowell House was built in 1767 and is known as Elmwood. James Russell Lowell, who was born and died on this estate, said that the "old mansion is a complete Temple of the Winds to which Aeolus's Cave was as calm as a maiden's dream." Built as one of the grandest estates on Tory Row, the house is now the residence of the dean of the Harvard faculty.

James Russell Lowell (1819–1891) was photographed by Oliver Wendell Holmes in 1864, sitting beneath a tree on his Elmwood property. A noted humorist, author, and diplomat, Lowell was the editor of *The Bigelow Papers* and author of *A Fable for Critics*.

The Egyptian Gateway at Mount Auburn Cemetery is an impressive entrance to the first garden cemetery in the United States. Carved in granite, replicating the original that was built in wood, the gateway emulates examples in Denderah and Karnak in Egypt. Consecrated in 1831, the cemetery was designed as a picturesque landscape, planted with trees and shrubs and embellished with monuments, representing a revolutionary concept—one which was readily accepted by Bostonians.

Plans for the George Washington Tower at Mount Auburn Cemetery were drawn by Gridley J. Fox Bryant, from the design of Dr. Jacob Bigelow. Built in 1852 on the highest elevation in Mount Auburn, the crenelated tower of hammered Quincy granite rises 62 feet and affords a superb view of Boston and the surrounding towns.

The Chapel at Mount Auburn was designed by Dr. Jacob Bigelow, president of the cemetery from 1845 to 1871. It was built in 1843 as a striking Protestant Gothic granite chapel with soaring pinnacles that formed a spiked diadem surrounding the pitched roof. The chapel was deemed unsafe and was rebuilt in 1858.

Hazel Dell was a small secluded path with mausoleums built in the side of the embankment, or wooded dell. The aspect of working with natural features rather than changing them to suit the design made for a remarkably natural landscape dotted with funeral monuments.

The interior of the chapel at Mount Auburn Cemetery has been used for funerals and memorial services ever since it was built in 1843. Statues of John Winthrop (by Richard S. Greenough), John Adams (by Randolph Rogers), James Otis (by Thomas Crawford), and Judge Joseph Story (by his son William Wetmore Story) were placed in the chapel in the mid-19th century as representatives of four great periods in the history of Massachusetts. In 1934, the statues were given to Harvard University and can now be seen at the Harvard Law School and Memorial Hall.

This bucolic setting was the final resting place of Mary Baker Eddy, the founder of the Christian Science religion. The circular monument of white marble with columns supporting a classical lintel merged within the arboretum setting and became part of the whole rather than a singular site.

The sphinx was sculpted by Martin Milmore (1844–1883) and dedicated in 1872 to the preservation of the American Union and the destruction of African slavery. This Civil War monument was the gift of Dr. Jacob Bigelow. Its design reflected the mid-19th-century revival of Egyptian funereal sculpture and architecture.

Two
HARVARD SQUARE

Photographed in the summer of 1889, Harvard Square was a bustling intersection, with a Thomson-Houston electric car and trailer curving along Massachusetts Avenue and two horsecars approaching from the east. Harvard Square had already become a busy shopping area, with stores, banks, and offices along the streets facing Harvard Yard. On the right is Allnutt's Dining Rooms, with Little's Block, the highest building, in the center. On the far left can be seen a part of Harvard's Dane Hall, now the site of Lehman Hall. (Courtesy of Frank Cheney.)

Harvard Square in the decade prior to the Civil War was a bucolic crossroads with a few buildings that constituted commercial activity. Brattle Street runs west in the center, with the Lyceum Building on the right, the site of the Harvard Coop.

Photographed at the time of the Civil War, Harvard Square had majestic elm trees shading Massachusetts Avenue. On the right can be seen the wall of Harvard Yard, now the site of Lehman Hall. The horse-drawn streetcar heads north and passes the present site of the Out of Town Newspapers stand.

A Broadway-bound streetcar awaits its horse in Harvard Square in the mid-1880s. In the rear is College House, a dormitory for Harvard students, with shops on the first floor. On the far right can be seen the First Parish Church of Cambridge. (Courtesy of Frank Cheney.)

Looking down Massachusetts Avenue in the late 19th century from the site of the Harvard Coop, a group of passengers stand in the center of the avenue, waiting to board a streetcar. The building on the right, with horizontal stringcourses, is Little's Block. (Courtesy of Frank Cheney.)

College House was built on Massachusetts Avenue, across from Harvard Yard. The Harvard Square post office and Harvard dormitories were located in this block.

Little's Block, on the right, was a red brick and limestone building that had college dormitories at the turn of the century. Built in 1854 by Charles Coffin Little, it was enlarged in 1869 for additional accommodations and given a new facade in 1877. A corner of Harvard Yard can be seen on the left.

Holyoke House had stores on the first floor, including the University Bookstore, with dormitory suites above. The fashionable mansard roof allowed further living space while creating an impressive and uniform design. On the right can be seen Little's Block. The entire block was demolished in 1961, and a high-rise office building was built on the site.

The Hilton Block was a fashionable dormitory that was built by James Manter Hilton. Located on Harvard Street between Holyoke and Linden Streets, the building included on its first-floor Leavitt & Pierce's Billiard Parlor, an office of the Cambridge Gas Company, a hairdressing salon, and a tailor shop.

This mid-19th-century photograph shows the First Parish Unitarian Church from a corner of Harvard Yard. Built in 1833 by the noted architect Isaiah Rogers, the wood-framed church had elaborate, Gothic decorative trim that has since been removed.

Massachusetts Hall, built between 1718 and 1720, was an early dormitory for Harvard College. This mid-19th-century photograph shows the building, with the First Parish Unitarian Church on the right. The juxtaposition of the early-Georgian red brick building and the wood-framed Gothic church creates an interesting contrast.

By 1912, Harvard Square had evolved into a bustling hub of activity, with a circular brick subway entrance rising from the center of the square. Between two columns, which support the kiosk roof, well-dressed passengers wait for a streetcar. The Wadsworth House can be seen in the distance, just to the left of the streetcars on Massachusetts Avenue.

The center of this panorama of Harvard Square shows the kiosk of the Cambridge-to-Boston Subway (the present Red Line), the Harvard Cooperative Society, College House, and the spire of the First Parish Unitarian Church.

By 1929, Harvard Square had changed once more. The circular brick kiosk had been replaced in 1928 by a copper-vaulted kiosk, which took up less room and was not considered a traffic hindrance. The classical-style Cambridge Saving Bank, designed by Newhall and Blevins in 1923, stood between Dunster Street on the left and the 1896 Richards Block on the corner of Boylston Street.

This view looking north on Massachusetts Avenue from the Cambridge Saving Bank shows a throng of people emerging from the original circular brick kiosk of the Cambridge-to-Boston Subway. In the distance, on the right, are Massachusetts Hall and Hemenway Gymnasium. (Courtesy of Frank Cheney.)

Harvard Square looks deserted on this early Sunday morning in the 1920s, as a streetcar passes the subway entrance. On the left is College House, and in the distance is the Hemenway Gymnasium cupola. (Courtesy of Frank Cheney.)

Lehman Hall, a gift of Arthur Lehman, was built in 1924 between Massachusetts Avenue and Harvard Yard. Shown here on the right, it was designed by the architectural firm of Coolidge, Shepley, Bulfinch, and Abbott. It was erected during a massive building boom that occurred under Harvard President Abbott Lawrence Lowell, as was Straus Hall, on the left. Rising above these buildings is the spire of Memorial Church, a 1931 church that was designed in the style of Boston's Christ Church (Old North Church) by Coolidge, Shepley, Bulfinch, and Abbott. On the left is the roof tower of Memorial Hall.

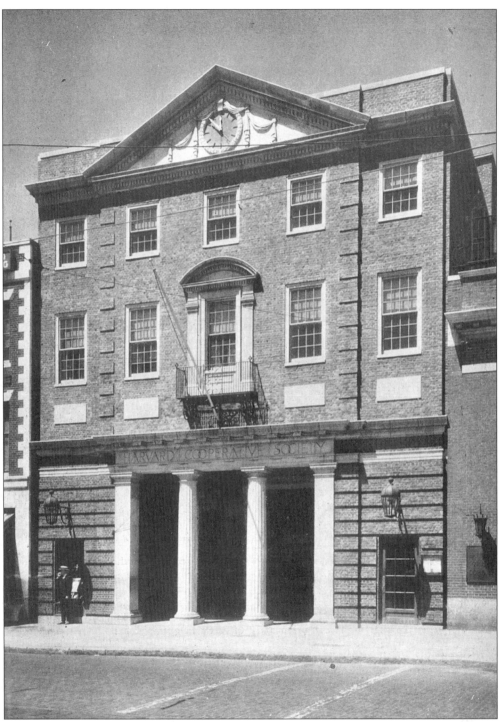

The new building of the Harvard Cooperative Society was designed by the noted architectural firm of Perry, Shaw, and Hepburn. It was built in 1924 on the site of the original society, just to the left of College House. The Harvard Coop was a place where one could purchase everything from books and bedding to linens and towels.

Three
THE CITY OF
CAMBRIDGE

Members of the 1930–31 Cambridge Rindge High School Basketball Team pose for a photograph with manager Thomas J. Murphy, left rear, and assistant manager Eddie Moynahan, rear right. The team captain was John E. Deluise, seated in the center and holding the basketball.

The seal of Cambridge has Gore Library of Harvard College with the word *Cantabrigia* below. Cambridge was so named in 1638, having been known as New Towne for the previous eight years. Cambridge became a city in 1846. It is the seat of Middlesex County.

The first mayor of Cambridge was the Rev. James D. Green (1798–1882). A well-respected clergyman, Green "set the example of uprightness, ability, and faithful work" and began the high standards which his successors have endeavored to uphold. Green served the city as mayor in 1846–47, 1853, and 1860–61.

Cambridge City Hall was a gift to the city from Frederick H. Rindge, a former Cambridge resident who lived in California. Built in 1890 on Massachusetts Avenue, between Bigelow and Inman Streets at Central Square, it replaced the old city hall that was located in the former Cambridge Athenaeum. The new city hall was designed by Longfellow, Alden, and Harlow. With its quarry-faced stone and 154-foot tower, it was an impressive part of the streetscape.

Frederick H. Rindge was a generous benefactor to the city of Cambridge in the late 19th century. A man who was said to be of "ample fortune and of generous impulses," Rindge said of his own generosity that "What I am aiming to do is to establish certain didactic public buildings." The buildings may not actually have been didactic, but the morally uplifting words he had carved into the stone certainly were.

The laying of the cornerstone of the Cambridge City Hall was held on May 15, 1889, with the Most Worshipful Henry Endicott, grand master of the Grand Lodge of Masons of Massachusetts, officiating. Thousands of interested citizens and the outright curious turned out to witness this momentous occasion.

The new Cambridge City Hall had a terraced setback from Massachusetts Avenue. The quarry-faced stone building measured 157 feet in length and 92 feet deep and had a tower that was 27 feet square and 154 feet high. A massive and impressive building, it was the gift of Frederick H. Rindge.

Members of the Cambridge Police Department of 1880 pose in front of police headquarters. The first police force in 1846 was composed of one night policeman with the ironic name of Day, seven constables, and seven watchmen. Within five decades, the force had grown to include a chief of police, 3 captains, 1 inspector, 8 sergeants, and 82 patrolmen—a far cry from the force of today.

Members of the Cambridge Police Department of 1915 pose on the steps of police headquarters in Central Square. From three constables in 1845, the Cambridge Police Department has grown into a professional department serving a major city.

In the mid-1880s, the fire and police stations of East Cambridge were side by side. Some of the engines in the mid-19th century included Cambridge no. 1 on Church Street, Union no. 2 in Cambridgeport, Niagara no. 3 in East Cambridge, and Daniel Webster no. 4 in North Cambridge. Engine no. 4 (above), a horse-drawn chemical engine, was photographed with the firefighters assigned to this firehouse at 4 Russell Street in the late 1890s. Notice the police station on the left.

Members of Ladder Company 3, the Lafayette Square Fire Station, pose with their horses and ladder truck.

This 1914 photograph shows Engine Company 5, the first motorized equipment in the fire department.

The new Cambridge Public Library was built in 1889 on a lot bounded by Cambridge, Trowbridge, and Irving Streets and Broadway. Like the new City Hall, it was a gift to the city from Frederick H. Rindge. Designed by Van Brunt and Howe, the Romanesque-revival building has a soaring tower separating a dual-arched entrance from the reading room.

The first librarian of the Cambridge public library system was Caroline Frances Orne, who served from 1858 to 1874. Founded in 1849, the Cambridge Athenaeum was incorporated for the purpose of establishing a lyceum, library, and reading room. However, it was not until 1857 that the library was opened to the public. Known originally as the Dana Library, it became known as the Cambridge Public Library in 1879.

The interior of the Cambridge Public Library had an art gallery that opened to the reference reading room.

The delivery room is an impressive space, which had wood benches where patrons sat while waiting for books to be brought to them from the stacks. The five tablets above the delivery desk were engraved with words by Frederick H. Rindge that expounded the virtues of what constituted a good citizen.

An American flag-bedecked float in the Tercentenary Parade of Cambridge in 1930 had young ladies bearing torches of knowledge, with a larger-than-life book open and ready to be read. The library can be seen on the left; as the city grew, branch libraries were established in East Cambridge in 1897, North Cambridge in 1906, Central Square in 1913, and Cambridge Field and Mount Auburn in 1915.

The children's room, which had juvenile periodicals and books, was packed in this 1907 photograph. At the turn of the century, schoolchildren knew about the library and its collections from school visits by librarians. Encouraged to use the children's room, students often studied in the library after school.

The Cambridge Hospital was photographed in 1906 from the rear, which had a 500-foot waterfront along the Charles River. From the far left are the Nurses' Home, the Men's Ward, the Administration Building, the Women's Ward, and the Operating Building.

The Cambridge Municipal Hospital was built on Cambridge Street and was an impressive Colonial-revival building with a two-story portico. (Courtesy of the Cambridge Health Alliance.)

Nurses and doctors of the Cambridge Municipal Hospital pose around a float that was in a parade in 1946 celebrating the 100th anniversary of Cambridge being a city.

50

The Cambridge Public Library, on the left, the Latin and English High Schools were an impressive assemblage on this postcard from the early 20th century.

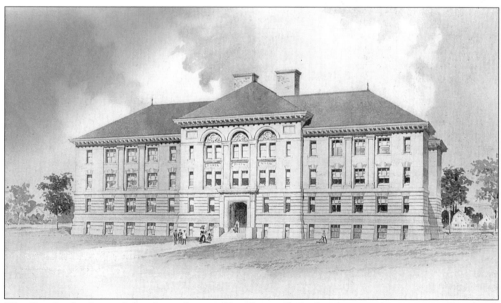

The Cambridge Latin School was designed by Hartwell, Richardson, and Driver in yellow brick and was built in 1898 at the corner of Broadway and Fayette Street. The school was established in 1886 when the Cambridge High School, founded in 1838, was divided into two schools: the classical department became Cambridge Latin and the remaining departments became the Cambridge English High School.

51

The Cambridge English High School was designed by Chamberlain and Austin and was built in 1892 on Broadway, between Trowbridge and Ellery Streets. Notice the Cambridge Public Library on the far left. This is now the site of the Cambridge High and Latin School, designed by Charles R. Greco and built in 1939.

Saint Paul's Church was built in 1915 at the intersection of Bow and Arrow Streets. Designed by Edward T.P. Graham, the Italian-Romanesque-style church includes a campanile that is a distinctive feature and local landmark.

The Cambridge Manual Training School was designed in Romanesque-revival style by the architectural firm of Rotch and Tilden. Founded and given to the city by Frederick H. Rindge in 1888, the school was built at the corner of Broadway and Irving Street. The industrial school taught carpentry, blacksmithing, iron fitting, and mechanical drawing. Notice the tower of Memorial Hall on the far left.

The Blacksmith Shop at the Cambridge Manual Training School had a group of students learning the trade of smithing in this photograph from early 1900s. Notice the floor anvils that the students hammered their metals on.

Members of the fire brigade at the Cambridge Manual Training School practice a fire drill with canvas hoses and ladders. Students unroll the canvas hose from a two-wheeled roller on the right while others place ladders on the side of the school. "Presence of mind in emergencies is a marked result of fire drill, as well as the development of the finer qualities of respect to superiors, obedience, courage, and tact in managing others" was a motto of the school.

A group of students sit at drafting tables in the drawing room of the Cambridge Manual Training School. The drafting instructor stands at the left of the double doors, offering assistance to the students drawing line perspectives. Rindge Technical High School, designed by Ralph H. Doane and built in 1932, is now on the site of the Cambridge Manual Training School.

Four
CANTABRIGIA

Harvard Street runs from Main Street to Harvard Square. The large Italianate house on the left, *c.* 1870, is indicative of the building boom in Cambridge in the post Civil War years. With houses springing up, as if by magic, Cambridge was fast attracting a well-to-do middle class of citizens.

Sarah Margaret Fuller (1810–1850), well-known reformer, writer, and transcendentalist, was born on Cherry Street in Cambridgeport. A frequent visitor to the utopian community Brook Farm, she extolled the virtues of free thought and utopian ideals and was often referred to as the Priestess of Transcendentalism. After her marriage to the Marquis d'Ossoli, she lived abroad. She died with her husband and infant when the ship they were aboard was wrecked off the harbor of New York.

Craigie Street runs from Brattle Street to Concord Avenue. Photographed c. 1895, the tree-lined street had a bucolic air with an arching passage of overhanging branches extending the length of the street. The street was named for Andrew Craigie, a real estate speculator and Brattle Street resident.

Col. Thomas Wentworth Higginson (1823–1911) and his daughter Margaret (Mrs. James Dellinger Barney) pose for their photograph astride a three-wheeled bicycle. Higginson was the first colonel of a black regiment in the Civil War and was the author of *Army Life in a Black Regiment*, *Atlantic Essays*, *Common Sense About Women*, *The Afternoon Landscape*, and numerous other books. His essay in the *Atlantic Monthly* entitled "Ought Women to Learn the Alphabet?" was so thought provoking that it is credited as the seed from which Smith College grew.

The Higginson House was a large shingle-style house built at 29 Buckingham Street. Thomas W. Higginson and his wife, Mary Channing Higginson, can be seen near the dining room windows admiring a flower bed.

Alexander Agassiz (1835–1910) was the son of naturalist Louis Agassiz. Following his graduation from Harvard in 1855, he became superintendent of the Calumet and Hecla mines, developing them until they became the most prolific ore bearers ever known. He increased the capacity of the Agassiz Museum of Comparative Zoology, which his father had founded. It was said that he was "the best authority in the world on certain forms of marine life."

Maj. Gen. William A. Bancroft graduated from Harvard in 1878 and later attended Harvard Law School. Associated with the Cambridge Railroad, he was appointed general road master of the West End Street Railway. He eventually became president of the Boston Elevated Railway and later served as mayor of Cambridge. He and his wife, Mary Shaw Bancroft, lived in Arborcroft, at 12 Ware Street.

The Marean House at 151 Brattle Street was a large Colonial-revival house built by Joseph Mason Marean (1849–1909). It had an exuberance of overblown classical detail, which had its basis in the Colonial period but was in no way architecturally correct. (Courtesy of the Milton Historical Society, with thanks to Barbara W. Stebbins.)

Washington Avenue, which runs from Linnaean Street to Upland Road, was developed with large houses in the 1870–90 period. This c. 1895 photograph shows houses on Washington Avenue, all built on large, open lots with a uniform setback from the street. The houses on the left front onto Avon Hill.

The Eliot House, also known as the president's house at Harvard College, was built in 1861 with a gift to the college from Peter Chardon Brooks. A brick house with a slate Mansard roof, it was located on Quincy Street. Notice the twin spires of Gore Library on the left.

Charles W. Eliot (1834–1926) graduated from Harvard College in 1853, became a professor of chemistry, and was elected president of Harvard in 1869. He was "identified with the highest and worthiest movements for the public good." After his retirement as president of Harvard, he served as president emeritus from 1909 to 1926 and lived at 17 Fresh Pond Parkway.

The Edwin Hale Abbot House was designed by Longfellow, Alden, and Harlow and was built in 1889. The impressive granite house at 1 Follen Street is now the Longey School of Music and includes concert-hall and library additions designed by Huygens and Tappe.

Charles Eliot Norton (1827–1908) was considered to be one of this country's foremost arbiters of elegant taste in the late 19th century. A critic, author, and professor of art history at Harvard, he was erudite, cultured, and the translator of *Dante* to English.

The Van Brunt House was built in 1883 at 167 Brattle Street. Designed by owner Henry Van Brunt, the large Queen Anne house has many gables, turned porch posts, and shingle designs, which make it eclectic Victorian.

Arthur Elmer Denison (1847–1916) was educated at Tufts College and was admitted to the Suffolk bar in 1874. Considered a "well-equipped lawyer, a man of culture and refinement," he was often urged to run for mayor of Cambridge, which he steadfastly refused. Of him was said that "No one who knew him can ever fail to remember him with sincere and affectionate regard."

The Stoughton-Fiske-Paine House was designed by Henry Hobson Richardson and was built in 1883 at the corner of Brattle and Ash Streets for Mary Fiske Green Stoughton. A large shingle-style house, it combined classical interior details with the prevalent style so favored by Richardson—rounded stair hall, open balcony, and massive roof.

John Fiske, born Edmund Fiske Green (1842–1900), graduated from Harvard College in 1863 and became a noted philosopher, historian, and lecturer. His study of the doctrine of evolution brought him immediate prominence and in 1871, he made his remarkable discovery of the effects of the prolongation of infancy in bringing about the development of man from a lower creature.

Josephine Preston Peabody (1874–1922) lived at 192 Brattle Street from 1911 to 1922. A noted poet and writer, she was able to create the impression of realism using the printed word. She once wrote "I am wildly happy while I am doing it, though it doesn't for a moment dull the longing after color; and shan't neither!" She was photographed in 1911 with her children Alison and Lionel. Her husband was Lionel Marks, a professor of engineering at Harvard.

Beulah Marie Dix graduated from the Harvard Annex (Radcliffe) in 1897 and later wrote *Soldier Rigdale*, *The Making of Christopher Ferringham*, and *A Little Captive Lad*. She lived with her family at 77 Larch Road as somewhat of a recluse, never traveling far from home, until 1917 when she moved to California to write plays for motion pictures.

Irving Street runs from Kirkland Street to Francis Avenue on the "Somerville Fringe," as it was referred to in the late 1800s These substantial Colonial-revival houses were built on Irving Street in the last decade of the 19th century.

Bliss Perry (1860–1954), well-known educator and critic, was a professor of English literature at Harvard for 19 years. Perry graduated from Williams College and became a professor of English there. Later, he served as chair of the English department at Princeton, before being appointed editor of the *Atlantic Monthly*.

Posing on the side lawn of 908 Massachusetts Avenue (now demolished) in 1903 were, from left to right, Arthur D. Wyman, Ellie Chapman, Florence Wyman, Charles F. Wyman, and Helen Wyman. In his book *The Bostonians*, Henry James describes this stretch of Massachusetts Avenue as being "fringed on either side with villas offering themselves trustfully to the public," and "the detatched [sic] houses had, on top, little cupolas and belvederes, in front pillared piazzas."

Some boys pose on the rear steps of the Wyman House at 908 Massachusetts Avenue in the late 1800s after a baseball game, a tennis game, or a bicycle race, as all three sports are represented in the photograph. Arthur Wyman, who lived in this house, is in the rear on the far right.

Five

CENTRAL SQUARE,
CAMBRIDGEPORT, AND
EAST CAMBRIDGE

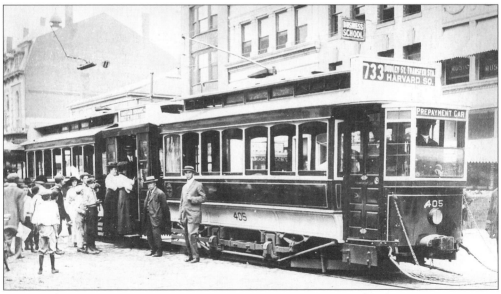

Service on today's Green Line in Boston is supplied by modern articulated cars, as it is on many light-rail systems worldwide. The articulated design enables cars to bend in the middle as they go around corners. The now popular design was developed in May 1912 by John Lindall, chief equipment engineer of the Boston Elevated Company, one of whose early articulated cars is seen here on Massachusetts Avenue at Central Square, en route to Dudley Street in Roxbury. (Courtesy of Frank Cheney.)

Central Square presents a busy scene in this early-1920s view looking toward Harvard Square. An early type of articulated car, often referred to as a snake car, is loading passengers destined for Union Square in Somerville, as a long-vanished Selden motortruck passes by. Notice the tower of Cambridge City Hall rising in the center. (Courtesy of Frank Cheney.)

The Old Hovey Tavern was located in Lafayette Square, the junction of Main Street and Massachusetts Avenue, and was a popular stopping point for travelers heading to or from Boston along Massachusetts Avenue. On the far right, partially hidden by a tree, is the First Universalist Church of Cambridge.

Thomas Dowse (1772–1856) was a leather dresser by trade and a bibliophile by occupation. His house, built in 1814, still stands at 653–655 Massachusetts Avenue in Central Square. His extensive library, now in the collection of the Massachusetts Historical Society, was thought to be the finest private library in Cambridge in the mid-19th century. (Collection of the Massachusetts Historical Society.)

The First Baptist Church was built in 1866 in Central Square. Destroyed by fire in 1881, it was replaced the same year by the present church, designed by Hartwell and Richardson.

The Cambridge Mutual Fire Insurance Company was organized in 1833. In 1888, the company built this Romanesque pattern brick building, designed by John A. Hasty, at the corner of Massachusetts Avenue and Inman Street. The First Universalist Church, now Saint Mary's Syrian Church, can be seen on the left. Notice the houses to the right on Massachusetts Avenue.

Members of the Cambridgeport Cycle Club pose *c.* 1890 at the corner of Massachusetts Avenue and Pearl Street in Central Square. The bicycle had been popularized by Albert A. Pope, who manufactured them in the late 19th century. Notice the members and friends of the club on the roof on the right, directly below the club's banner.

Two horse-drawn streetcars passing the First Universalist Church in Lafayette Square, the junction of Main Street and Massachusetts Avenue. The church was built in 1822 and was moved in 1888 to 8 Inman Street, adjacent to the Cambridge Mutual Fire Insurance Company. The church later became Saint Mary's Syrian Church, after which its spire was shorn.

Following World War I, many street railway companies were near bankruptcy and were seeking to reduce operating costs. Charles Birney, an engineer with Stone & Webster in Boston, designed the lightweight, one-man-operated Birney Safety Car. Purchased in large numbers by the Boston Elevated and Eastern Massachusetts Street Railway Systems, these cars proved impractical and were rapidly sold off. This Birney Safety Car was photographed in 1922 on Massachusetts Avenue in Central Square, opposite the Fisher Business College. (Courtesy of Frank Cheney.)

This 1905 photograph was taken from the corner of Brookline Street, looking along Massachusetts Avenue toward Harvard Square. The open trolley on the right is en route to Harvard Square and eventually Arlington Heights. The crowd standing on the left is waiting for a trolley to Boston or Roxbury. The tall building in the center is the Odd Fellows Hall, designed by Hartwell and Richardson and built in 1884. (Courtesy of Frank Cheney.)

Moller's Furniture Store dominated the south side of Central Square, as seen in this 1907 photograph. The two hip-roofed houses to the left of Moller's are indicative of the early-19th-century residences that once lined Massachusetts Avenue. (Courtesy of Frank Cheney.)

This 1907 view looking north on Massachusetts Avenue shows Central Square as a quiet intersection with horse-drawn vehicles making deliveries to various stores. Hyde's Block is on the far right. (Courtesy of Frank Cheney.)

Halfway between Harvard Square and the Charles River at the junction of Magazine Street is Central Square, on the right. The commercial buildings date from the last quarter of the 19th century, when this area along Massachusetts Avenue saw tremendous development. Hyde's Block is on the left.

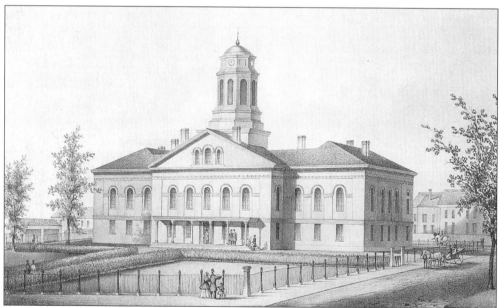

The Middlesex County Courthouse in East Cambridge was designed by the noted architect Charles Bulfinch (1763–1844), begun in 1814, and enlarged in 1848 by Ammi Burnham Young (1800–1874). Originally covered in stucco that was scored to imitate stone, the brick was added in an 1898 remodeling. The complex was recently restored by Graham Gund and Associates and is an attractive part of the development of the neighborhood.

The New England Glass Works in East Cambridge was etched for *Gleason's Pictorial Drawing Room Companion* in 1851. By the mid-19th century, the company was said to be the largest glass manufacturer in the world. In 1846, the glassworks employed 450 hands, had a capacity of 2,000 pounds to the pot, and produced glass with heat from furnaces named the Etna, the Vesuvius, and the Trio.

Edmund H. Munroe (1780–1865) was an incorporator of the New England Glass Company, which was incorporated on February 16, 1818. Along with Amos Binney, Daniel Hastings, and Deming Jarvis, Monroe was privileged to manufacture "flint and crown glass of all kinds in the towns of Boston and Cambridge." A former director of the Boston Porcelain & Glass Company, Monroe was a wealthy banker, broker, and China-trade investor whose involvement ensured the success of the new glass company.

The glass-blowing department of the New England Glass Company was etched for the January 20, 1855 edition of *Gleason's Pictorial Drawing Room Companion*. The room had a brick floor with a groined roof, supported by iron columns. It contained "four large furnaces and the annealing leers and kilns, and was the center of activity for the blowing, pressing, and finishing" of the glass.

The glass-cutting room of the New England Glass Company was etched for the January 20, 1855 edition of *Gleason's Pictorial Drawing Room Companion*. The 270-foot-long room contained 80 frames for cutting, polishing, and engraving glass. Some 90 men operated the 80-horsepower steam engine, which cut the glass into multifaceted designs. The steam engine was installed by Corlis & Nightingale of Providence, Rhode Island.

A showroom of the New England Glass Company was photographed in 1875. The room was 140 feet long and high in proportion, with "compotes, decanters, vases, bottles, and more especially a great number of lamps, lanterns, and lamp chimneys" displayed for the often bewildered customers, who were amazed at the wide selection of glassware.

A close-up photograph of another showroom gives an example of the wide array of glassware that was manufactured by the New England Glass Company. Notice in the background the gasoliers, which often could be fitted with glass chimneys of different designs.

John H. Leighton (1786–1849), second from the right, and his family epitomized the skilled workers and their families whose involvement with the New England Glass Company ensured its continued success. Born in England, Leighton was induced to emigrate to this country as a gaffer in 1826. His involvement with the New England Glass Company lasted until his death. Of his seven sons, five were glassblowers and one was a machinist in the mold shop—a remarkable glassworks family in East Cambridge.

The New England Glass Company set up an exhibit at the Centennial Exhibition in Philadelphia in 1876, with elaborate examples of cut glassware, chandeliers, and tableware—with all the cutting the pieces would bear. So popular was the exhibit that "a new market was created by the visitors who came from all parts of the country" and marveled at the designs.

The Prospect Congregational Church was built in 1851 on Prospect Street. Designed by Alexander R. Esty, the Romanesque-revival church had an exterior that was covered in mastic and scored to imitate ashlar masonry. A vestry designed by Thomas Silloway was added to the rear of the church in 1879.

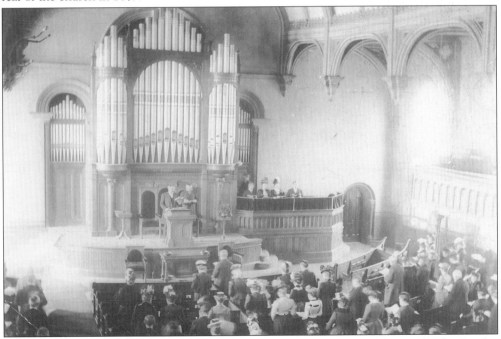

The interior of the Prospect Congregational Church was packed to overflowing for this Sunday Service in the 1890s.

Saint John's Church on Fourth Street in East Cambridge was built in 1842 and served as the first Roman Catholic church in Cambridge. An impressive stone church with a crenelated tower, Saint John's was built as a result of the large influx of Roman Catholic laborers to the numerous industries located in East Cambridge.

The Savings Bank Building was built in 1904 at 689 Massachusetts Avenue. The Cambridgeport Savings Bank and the Harvard Trust Company shared space in this impressive beaux arts building, designed by W.E. Chamberlin and Clarence H. Blackall.

Six
NORTH CAMBRIDGE

Massachusetts Avenue, originally known as North Avenue, was a winter wonderland in this late-19th-century photograph. Horse-drawn sleighs pass a streetcar heading north from Porter Square, with snow-bedecked tree branches arching overhead. The Arlington Heights-bound trolley has the street all to itself except for the three sleighs and two pedestrians brave enough to venture out of doors on this wintry day. (Courtesy of Frank Cheney.)

Chester Ward Kingsley was an active developer of North Cambridge in the late 19th century. Treasurer of an anthracite coal company in Pennsylvania, Kingsley devoted a large portion of his wealth and time to beautify and develop North Cambridge. As chairman of the committee that carried the metropolitan sewerage bill for the Valleys of the Charles and Mystic Rivers through the legislature, he was an influential proponent for the future of North Cambridge.

The Queen Anne–style residences of Horace Partridge and Frank P. Partridge were built at 1718 Massachusetts Avenue (below left) and 1722 Massachusetts Avenue (below right). The Partridges were partners in the Horace Partridge Company, wholesalers of fancy goods at 55 Hanover Street in Boston's North End and of sporting goods at 335 Washington Street in downtown Boston.

Saint James's Church was designed by Henry M. Congdon of New York. The church is located at the corner of Massachusetts Avenue and Beech Street, on the site of the Old Davenport Tavern. The cornerstone was laid in 1888 and the church opened for worship a year later, in November 1889. The chancel was given by Mrs. James Greenleaf as a memorial to her husband. An interesting feature of this church is the bell: the first bell cast by Paul Revere (1735–1818) hangs in the bell tower.

The men and boys' choir of Saint James's Church posed for a group photograph in 1900.

Notre Dame de Pitie was the French Roman Catholic Church on Harvey Street in North Cambridge. An impressive wood-framed church with flanking canopied piers, it was the first French Catholic church in the Boston area, and its first pastor was the Rev. Elphege Godin. The present church was designed by Charles R. Greco and was built in 1920 at 170 Rindge Avenue.

Andrew J. Lovell built the Lovell's Block at 1847–1853 Massachusetts Avenue to house not just the Andrew J. Lovell Company and the A.J. Littlefield & Company, provision dealers, but also the North Cambridge post office. An impressive panel brick commercial block, it had offices on the second and third floors.

ST. JOHN'S CHURCH, NORTH CAMBRIDGE, MASS.

Saint John the Evangelist Church was designed by Maginnis, Walsh, and Sullivan and was built between 1904 and 1912. Located at 2260 Massachusetts Avenue on the corner of Hollis Street, the church is an impressive example of the Italian-Romanesque style. The arcade along the facade and the soaring campanile are distinctive features. The church was rebuilt after a 1956 fire by Maginnis, Walsh, and Kennedy, the successor to the original builder.

3983. - St. John's Church (Cath.), Interior, NORTH CAMBRIDGE, Mass.

This interior view of Saint John's Church shows composite columns supporting a barrel-vaulted ceiling, which extends the length of the nave. A beautiful stained glass window depicting the Crucifixion rises above a high marble altar with rich Byzantine decorations. One of the treasurers of the church is a magnificent gold monstrance.

A horse-drawn omnibus, which connected Boston and Cambridge via Harvard Street, passes Dane Hall. This elegant Greek-revival building was built in 1832 and was enlarged in 1845. Named for Nathan Dane, a noted jurist and statesman, Dane Hall served as the first edifice of the Harvard Law School. It was located on the site of Lehman Hall in Harvard Square.

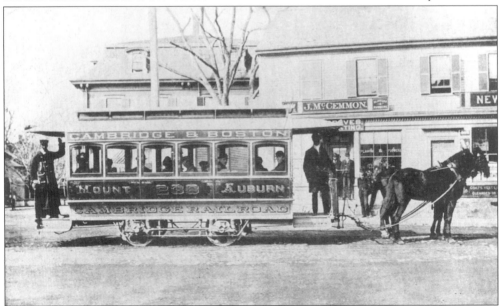

In this c. 1880 photograph, the conductor on the rear platform sounds the starting bell on the horsecar heading from Mount Auburn in Cambridge to Scollay Square in downtown Boston. Electric cars took over this route in 1889 and were replaced by electric trolleybuses as far as Harvard Square. (Courtesy of Frank Cheney.)

Seven
ALL MODES OF
TRANSPORTATION

In 1924, eager passengers board a Massachusetts Avenue Fageol Safety Coach, used on the route from Central Square in Cambridge to the Cottage Farm Bridge. Frank Fageol was one of the pioneer bus manufacturers in the United States, and his company remained in business until *c*. 1960. (Courtesy of Frank Cheney.)

It is March 1888, and this rather shabby looking horsecar of the Cambridge Railroad stands at the waiting room in Harvard Square on the corner of Dunster Street, having just arrived from Boston. Less than a year later, this route was operating with the newly developed electric cars, which eliminated the need for horses. (Courtesy of Frank Cheney.)

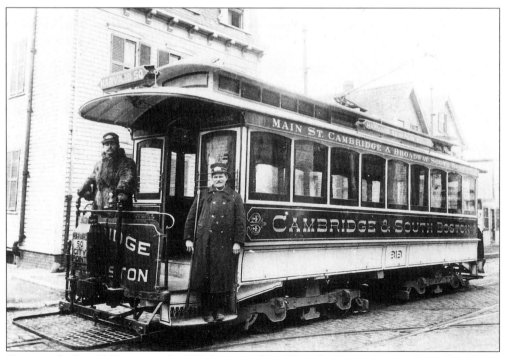

Photographed in 1892 is a standard 25-foot car of the West End line, about to leave City Point in South Boston for Harvard Square in Cambridge. Just over 1,100 of these standard cars carried passengers from 1891 to 1928. Notice the oil headlight and the motorman's coat of heavy fur—warm enough to keep out the cold winter winds. (Courtesy of Frank Cheney.)

A capacity test is being conducted at the Albany Street Shops of the West End Street Railway to determine how many passengers can be carried in a trolley car. After packing the car with burly workers, officials determined that every standing passenger was entitled to 1.7 square feet of space. The trolley car in this 1892 photograph is a rebuilt horsecar equipped for electric operation. (Courtesy of Frank Cheney.)

In the summer of 1892, crew members of this trolley on the long Bowdoin Square-Harvard Square-Arlington Heights line stopped long enough to have their picture taken on North Avenue. In 1901, a state law mandated closed ends for trolley cars, thereby providing protection from the cold weather for motormen, as car operators were called. (Courtesy of Frank Cheney.)

This photograph was taken on September 9, 1906, at the Cambridge end of the new West Boston Bridge and shows a trolley from Harvard Square heading for Scollay Square, amidst construction debris. The three gentlemen in front of the car are officials of the Boston Elevated Railway Company. (Courtesy of Frank Cheney.)

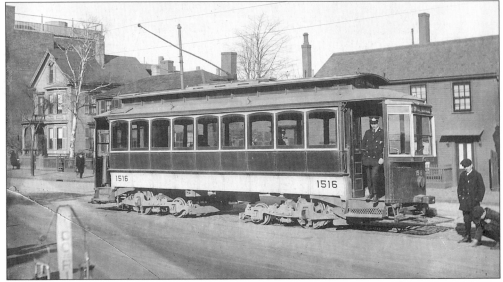

No one seems to be in a rush in this view of a trolley en route from Central Square to Cottage Farm Bridge. Trolley 1516 was built in 1899 by the Saint Louis Car Company, one of America's largest railcar builders until it closed in 1974. (Courtesy of Frank Cheney.)

On a warm sunny day in 1894, this open trolley heads for Harvard Square along Cambridge Street. This trolley was photographed at Warren Street, with a sewer construction project under way in the foreground. Note that many of the houses have their blinds shut, which allowed air to circulate while the hot sun was out—a common practice at the time. (Courtesy of Frank Cheney.)

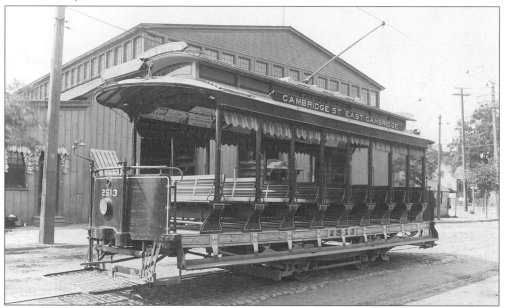

Standing in front of the Boylston Street Car House near Harvard Square in 1903 is Open Trolley 2513. This car provided Cambridge and Boston residents with comfortable summer transportation and was similar to more than 1,000 other open cars in service at the time. The last open trolleys were retired in 1919. (Courtesy of Frank Cheney.)

This 1932 view looking up Aberdeen Avenue from Mount Auburn Street shows a trolley waiting to depart for Harvard Square. Aberdeen Avenue is completely built up with residences and provides a neat, finished appearance. (Courtesy of Frank Cheney.)

A 1924 view of Aberdeen Avenue shows a trolley that has just arrived from Harvard Square via Huron Avenue. Note the rather open character of Aberdeen Avenue at the time, with only a few houses in evidence. On the left is the Collins/Mount Auburn Branch of the Cambridge Public Library. (Courtesy of Frank Cheney.)

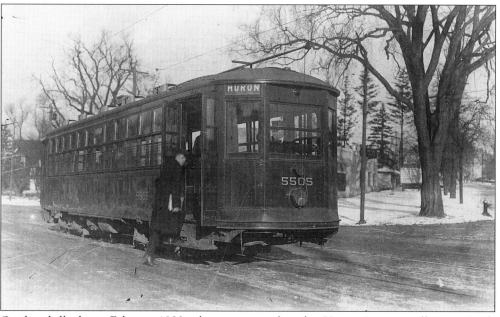

On this chilly day in February 1923, a lone passenger boards a Huron Avenue trolley near Fresh Pond Parkway. This car is one of the durable Type Five cars that served Cambridge residents from 1922 to 1958, when they were replaced by electric trolleybuses. (Courtesy of Frank Cheney.)

In this February 1941 scene, a Waverly-bound trolley passes the former Mount Auburn Car House, later the Big Bear Supermarket and now Star Market, on Mount Auburn Street between Homer and Aberdeen Avenues. On the right is Mount Auburn Cemetery. (Courtesy of Frank Cheney.)

This late-1898 view shows the enlarged North Cambridge Car House, with its handsome facade and large illuminated clock. This building was demolished in 1937 and the trolleys henceforth were stored out of doors. Today, this site is occupied by a modern MBTA trolleybus servicing facility. (Courtesy of Frank Cheney.)

This scene in the summer of 1931 finds a group of ladies in light summer hats and dresses about to board the trolley for Harvard Square, while workmen apply white paint to the safety island that afforded waiting trolley patrons safety from the swift auto traffic. These islands lined Massachusetts Avenue from Harvard Square to the Arlington line. (Courtesy of Frank Cheney.)

This view of Massachusetts Avenue, looking towards Porter Square from Harvard Square, was photographed in the spring of 1931. The gradual transition from large, private homes to large apartment buildings was slowly changing the character of this stretch of Massachusetts Avenue. (Courtesy of Frank Cheney.)

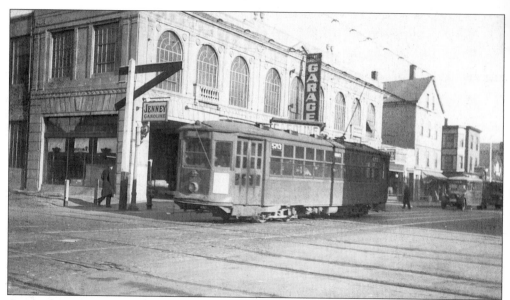

Cambridge Street was always a busy transit route. On this chilly winter day in 1935, a Harvard Square trolley, followed by a bus bound for Inman Square, approaches the Grand Junction railroad crossing, a busy freight line serving many Cambridge industries. (Courtesy of Frank Cheney.)

This view of Cambridge Street near Inman Square was taken in May 1938. This interesting ethnic neighborhood has changed little over the years, and many of the buildings in this photograph are still standing and in use. (Courtesy of Frank Cheney.)

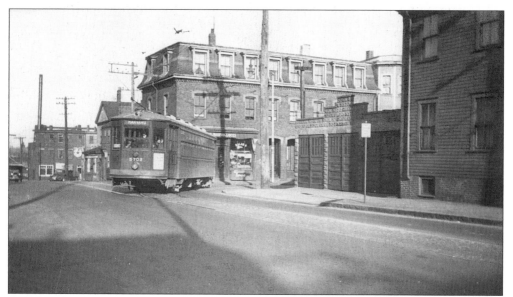

A Harvard Square-bound trolley turns onto Third Street, having just left Lechmere Square. Note the interesting mansard-roofed residence with the typical grocery store just behind the trolley. (Courtesy of Frank Cheney.)

At the corner of Massachusetts Avenue and Trowbridge Street on July 23, 1915, an open touring car with an impatient driver passes a summer trolley on the Pearl Street-Cottage Farm Bridge line. Granite paving blocks, typical in this period, are being used to repair the roadway. (Courtesy of Frank Cheney.)

A lone trolley deadheads out Concord Avenue toward Huron Avenue in this 1922 view, which is totally free of motor traffic except for the lone truck ahead of the trolley and one parked car. Ah, the good old days of the open roads of Cambridge! (Courtesy of Frank Cheney.)

This scene is at the North Cambridge Railroad Crossing on Massachusetts Avenue, looking outbound towards Arlington. Although photographed in 1931, there is still some horse-drawn trafficnote the wagon being passed by the Harvard Square-bound trolley. The gas station on the right is selling gas at 90 cents for seven gallons—what a bargain! (Courtesy of Frank Cheney.)

This August 1920 view is looking down Massachusetts Avenue toward Harvard Square from the Boston & Maine railroad crossing at North Cambridge. The rails at this heavily used crossing are being renewed. It is difficult to separate the workmen from the onlookers—concerns about liability were not a major factor at that time. (Courtesy of Frank Cheney.)

This interesting 1930 aerial view is looking north from the Charles River and the Harvard Boathouse along Boylston Street toward Harvard Square. Most of the land belongs to the Boston Elevated Railway Company, including from left to right, the Bennett Street Car House and train storage yard, the Eliot Square Rapid Transit Car Shops, and the company's Harvard Power Plant—now the site of Eliot House. All this property is now used for commercial and academic purposes. (Courtesy of Frank Cheney.)

Photographed in 1910, the Wadsworth House on Massachusetts Avenue faces excavations for the new subway of the Boston Elevated Railroad. Staging has been laid across the avenue, as workers excavate the tunnel that will connect Harvard Square in Cambridge and Boston. The Wadsworth House, built in 1726, was restored in 1912 following the excavation work and now serves as an alumni center of Harvard University. On the left is the pedimented red brick Lyceum Hall, just behind the crane, later the site of the Harvard Cooperative Society. (Courtesy of Frank Cheney.)

The Cambridge Subway was envisioned as running underground from Harvard Square to the Charles River and emerging on the Longfellow Bridge, which connected Cambridge and Boston. This 1910 photograph shows excavations under way on Massachusetts Avenue opposite the Wadsworth House—the beginning of the project that eventually connected Cambridge and Boston. In 1927, this line was extended to Ashmont in Dorchester in 1927. Today, it is known as the Red Line. (Courtesy of Frank Cheney.)

The Boston Elevated Railroad opened the subway connecting Harvard Square in Cambridge and Boston in 1912. This photograph taken that year shows a Boston-bound train on the Longfellow Bridge. The bridge was designed by Edmund March Wheelwright and built in 1890. It is often called the Salt and Pepper Bridge because of its uniquely shaped pavilions. The new campus of the Massachusetts Institute of Technology is visible in the center, on the Cambridge side of the Charles River.

Serving as employees of the Boston Elevated Railroad for 50 years or more, as of 1929, were, from left to right: (seated) Patrick Roach, James Kenney, A.L. Hauser, John Howard, Patrick J. Horan, William Pett, James Smith, Timothy Connell, Andrew Blake, Henry A. Bryant, Patrick H. Kelley, George W. Clark, John Sullivan; (standing) F.E. Hanington, C.H. Lewis, Robert E. Nelson, Patrick Donoghue, Richard J. Moore, T. Devine, Frank Holbrook, John Carl, C.I. Chadbourne, Frank P. Brown, Charles E. Sever, George E. Costello, Austin Shuttleworth, and George A. Gilman.

In April 1938, the Boston Elevated Company introduced speedy, quiet electric trolleybuses on the route from Harvard Square to Huron and Aberdeen Avenues. This photograph shows a Huron Avenue trolleybus in the Harvard Square Tunnel Station. Cambridge is still served by these smooth, quiet, fume-free vehicles. (Courtesy of Frank Cheney.)

This January 1964 view shows Brattle Street, with the Eliot Square Rapid Transit Shop in the center right and the buildings of Harvard University in the background. The former car shop area is now the site of Harvard's Kennedy School of Government. The cupola of Eliot House is visible in the center. Eliot House, designed by Coolidge, Shepley, Bulfinch and Abbott, was built in 1930, and was named for Charles W. Eliot, president of Harvard University from 1869 to 1909. Its cupola is a copy of that on city hall in New York City. (Courtesy of Frank Cheney.)

Eight
HARVARD, RADCLIFFE, AND MIT

Class Day at Harvard has always been a festive occasion, and never more so than in the late 1800s, as shown in this photograph. Here, family and friends of graduates promenade in Harvard Yard, beneath trees festooned with Japanese lanterns. Meanwhile, on the right just through the trees in front of University Hall, commencement exercises take place. In his book *The Prelude and the Play*, Rufus Mann mentions "the college yard with its spires, domes, towers, and dormitories."

The seated bronze statue of the Rev. John Harvard (1607–1638) was sculpted by Daniel Chester French and was originally placed at the west end of Memorial Hall, visible in the distance. Since 1924, the statue held a place of honor in front of University Hall in Harvard Yard.

There in red brick which softening time defies
Stand square and stiff the Muses' factories.
—Lowell

A 1726 engraving of Harvard College, by Burgis, shows Harvard Hall on the left, Stoughton Hall, and Massachusetts Hall. In 1765, Harvard Hall replaced the first structure of the college, built in 1672 with donations from various New England towns. Stoughton Hall was erected in 1700 through the generosity of William Stoughton, Class of 1650. Massachusetts Hall was built in 1718 at the expense of the Province of Massachusetts as a student dormitory.

Louis Agassiz (1807–1873) and Benjamin Pierce (1809–1880) pose for their photograph with a terrestrial globe in the late 1860s. Agassiz served as the chair of Natural History at the Lawrence Scientific School at Harvard from 1848 until his death. Pierce, a scientist and astronomer, was associated with the Harvard Observatory for more than four decades. (Courtesy of The Boston Athenaeum.)

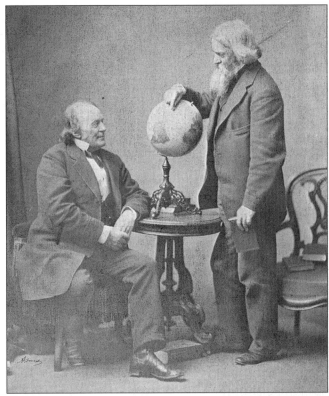

Five 19th-century presidents of Harvard College were photographed at the time of the Civil War. The presidents and their terms in office are, from left to right, Josiah Quincy, 1829 to 1845; Edward Everett, 1846 to 1849; James Walker, 1853 to 1860; Jared Sparks, 1849 to 1853; and Cornelius Conway Felton, 1860 to 1862.

Charles W. Eliot (1834–1926) was president of Harvard College from 1869 to 1909, during which time he recreated the college as a world-class university. Eliot House was built and named in his memory in 1930.

University Hall was designed by the noted architect Charles Bulfinch (1763–1844) as the first stone building erected in Harvard Yard. It was built in 1813 with a chapel, commons, and recitation rooms. The hall has seen many changes of occupancy but retains its strategic position in the quadrangle. Today, it contains the administrative offices of the Arts and Sciences faculty.

John Lovett was a well-known character at Harvard in the mid-19th century. A native of County Kerry, Lovett was known as "John the Orangeman." He achieved everlasting fame when he translated Harvard's *Veritas* as "Ter hell wid Yale!" He became a celebrity of sorts, a favored mascot at all athletic contests, and an ex officio member of every Harvard team, whether at the home grounds or on tour.

This photograph *c.* 1865 shows a "consistory of Goodies." The term Goody, an alternate of Goodwife, was used as early as the mid-1500s as a title preceding the surname of a woman of humble station. These Goodies were the chambermaids of the Harvard dormitories who went about their business "only in that chill hour when the rising-bell proclaims the truth of the dark saying—many are called, but few get up."

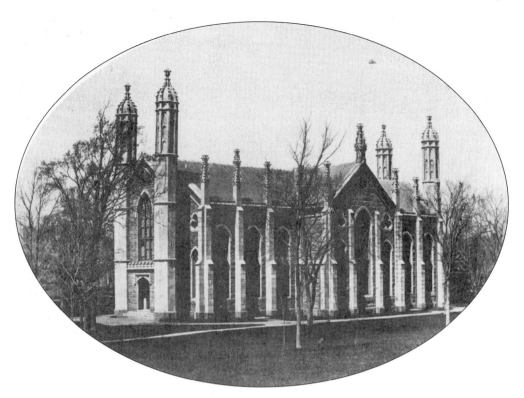

Gore Library was designed by Richard Bond as a Gothic library in the shape of a Latin cross, "a diminished copy of the chapel of King's College, at the greater Cambridge," according to noted author Henry James. The library was built in 1838 of Quincy granite, through a legacy made by Gov. Christopher Gore (1758–1827). It opened with 41,000 volumes and quickly grew to become the third largest library in the United States by the late 19th century. In 1874, the library was enlarged by Ware and Van Brunt. In 1912, it was demolished to make way for Widener Library.

Christopher Gore, the son of John and Frances Pinckney Gore, graduated from Harvard College in 1776. He served as governor of Massachusetts in 1809 and 1810, afterwards serving in the U.S. Senate from 1813 to 1816. Upon the death of his wife, Rebecca Amory Payne Gore (1759–1834), the Gore estate was donated to Harvard College, where Gore had served as a fellow of the corporation (1812–1821). The donation exceeded "the munificence of any other benefactor" up to that time.

Widener Library was built in 1915 on the site of Gore Library. The building was given to the university by Eleanor Elkins Widener in memory of her son Harry Elkins Widener, who lost his life in the sinking of the RMS *Titanic* in 1912. Built of red brick and Indiana limestone, the library was designed by Horace Trumbauer of Philadelphia with an impressive colonnade of Corinthian columns. Each year, on its imposing sweep of stairs, commencement exercises are held.

WIDENER LIBRARY, HARVARD UNIVERSITY. WIDENER COLLECTION

The Widener Collection, rare books collected by Harry Elkins Widener, was donated to the university by Eleanor Elkins Widener. A portrait of Harry Elkins Widener (1885–1912) hangs above the fireplace in this elegant Georgian-revival library.

The original observatory at Harvard College was designed by Isaiah Rogers (1800–1869) and built between 1844 and 1851 on Garden Street, Observatory Hill. A large central domed section was equipped with a powerful telescope, and two symmetrical wings flanked the dome on either side.

Adjacent to the observatory was a three-story house, which was built as the residence of William Cranch Bond (1789–1859), the first superintendent and a professor of astronomy from 1840 to 1858. Induced to move his home and observatory from Dorchester to Cambridge, Bond spent the remainder of his life studying the heavens from a lofty perch on Observatory Hill, just north of Harvard Square.

By 1900, the Astronomical Observatory of Harvard College had developed into a major observation site in the United States.

A group of women were photographed in the 1890s at the Harvard Observatory where they continued the work of Henry Draper, MD, LLD., in the study of the range of the spectrum. These women computed, made original deductions about, and kept catalogues of the spectra of stars.

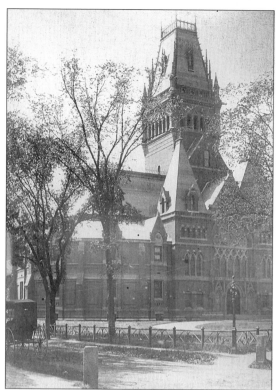

Memorial Hall was designed by Ware and Van Brunt as an impressive monument to Harvard's Civil War dead. Under construction from 1864 to 1878, the brick and Nova Scotia buff sandstone building was an impressive example of Ruskinian Gothicism. Its most striking feature was the massive tower that rose to a height of 200 feet. Memorial Hall was first used in 1874 at commencement.

Memorial Hall, the Memorial Transept, and Sanders Theatre constitute the three sections of this impressive Ruskinian Gothic structure called Memorial Hall. In Henry James's book *The Bostonians*, Memorial Hall is described as being as "Buttressed, cloistered, turreted, dedicated, superscribed, as he had never seen anything."

The dining hall on the west of Memorial Hall is 164 feet in length, 60 feet in width, and 80 feet in height and resembles a hall in an English college with its great hammer-beam trusses. The hall accommodates up to 1,000 diners at one seating and is a space that has never failed to create an impression.

Sanders Theatre was completed in 1876 on the east of Memorial Hall. It was named in memory of Charles Sanders, whose bequest helped fund construction. A central window of the balcony was designed by noted stained-glass artist John LaFarge and was given in memory of Cornelius Conway Felton (1807–1862), president of Harvard from 1860 to 1862.

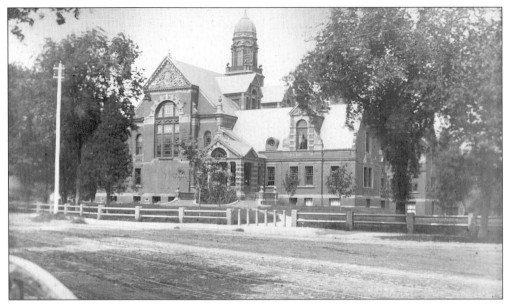

Hemenway Gymnasium was designed by Peabody and Stearns and was donated in 1878 to Harvard College by Augustus Hemenway of Boston and Milton. Known as the birthplace of the college "strong man," it was equipped with the then most up-to-date gymnasium equipment available and was staffed by an intelligent corps of instructors. The gymnasium was demolished in 1933.

Augustus Hemenway began his illustrious career in supercargo trading in the West Indies with a fleet of eight ships. Within a decade, Augustus Hemenway and Company began to invest its substantial trading profits in silver, copper, and nitrate mines in Chile, sawmills in Maine, and assorted commodities that were traded along the coast of South America. Hemenway's wife was Mary Porter Tileston Hemenway, a socially prominent woman who instituted domestic science classes in the Boston public schools during her tenure on the school committee.

The interior of the Hemenway
Gymnasium was 119 feet long and
52 feet high at the center ridge.
The interior had a large center hall,
a running gallery, dressing rooms,
bathing rooms, and meeting rooms
for the Harvard Athletic Association
and for the baseball, football,
gymnastic, and wrestling clubs.

Dr. Dudley A. Sargeant was the
director of the Hemenway
Gymnasium by the beginning of
the 20th century. Accepting the
position of assistant professor of
physical training at Harvard in
1879, he developed a "new system
of physical culture," which led
to a generation of gym-trained
young men.

Two cheerleaders of the late 1800s enthusiastically wave Harvard pennants.

On Class Day, June 16, 1914, members of the Harvard Class of 1864 marched to Harvard Stadium past the Weld Boathouse, which had been designed by Peabody and Stearns and built in 1907 through the generosity of George Walker Weld. Class members are, from left to right, James T. Bixby, Henry A. Parker, Edward Russell Cogswell, Woodward Emery, and Edward Blake Robins, holding the class flag.

Elizabeth Cabot Cary Agassiz (1822–1907) founded Radcliffe College in 1879 and became its first president. Originally known as the Harvard Annex, or the Society for the Collegiate Instruction of Women, the college was first located in a small wood-framed house on Appian Way. In 1885, it moved to Fay House, which was enlarged and adapted to suit the needs of the school. Radcliffe was formally incorporated in 1894 and was merged with Harvard University in 1999.

Fay House was built in 1807 by Nathaniel Ireland and was sold shortly thereafter to Judge Samuel Phillips Prescott Fay. The elegant neoclassical house at 10 Garden Street, opposite the Common, was sold by the Fay heirs to Radcliffe in 1885. In 1890, it was substantially remodeled for the college by Longfellow, Alden, and Harlow.

Students attend a lecture at one of the large recitation rooms at Radcliffe College c. 1890. The instructors at Radcliffe taught by the Harvard method, and "no instructor is employed who is not already connected with the University."

Fay House was enlarged between 1890 and 1892 by the architectural firm of Longfellow, Alden, and Harlow. The mansard roof was removed and a third story was added, but the elegance of the Colonial-revival building was maintained. The original entrance was on the far right.

The Radcliffe Quadrangle was photographed c. 1915. On the right is Fay House and on the left, the Radcliffe Gymnasium designed by McKim, Mead, and White and built in 1898. Rising between the two buildings is the spire of the Shepard Memorial Church. The church was designed by Abel C. Martin and built in 1870. Its 200-pound cockerel weathervane was wrought by Deacon Shem Drown in 1721 for the New Brick Meetinghouse on Hanover Street in Boston's North End.

The Elizabeth Cary Agassiz House was built in 1904 and was named in honor of the first president of Radcliffe. Designed by Alexander Wadsworth Longfellow Jr., its imposing Ionic portico creates an impressive focal point for the Quadrangle. On the right is the Radcliffe Gymnasium.

MASSACHUSETTS INSTITUTE OF TECHNOLOGY AND HARVARD BRIDGE, CAMBRIDGE, MASS.

This view, looking from Boston toward Cambridge, shows the Harvard Bridge spanning the Charles River and the Maclaurin Building on the Massachusetts Institute of Technology campus. Designed in 1913 by MIT graduate William Wells Bosworth of the Class of 1898, the building faces the river embankment. Its Roman dome and Ionic colonnade create a classical unity along Memorial Drive and the Charles River.

Richard Cockburn Maclaurin (1870–1920) was president of the Massachusetts Institute of Technology from 1909 to 1920. It was under his presidency that the college moved from the Back Bay of Boston to Cambridge.

The Great Court of the Massachusetts Institute of Technology is an impressive and monumental space that overlooks Boston and the north side of the Charles River. The grand design in light-colored limestone, creates a total effect with the domed central pavilion and the symmetrical flanking wings.

Riverbank Court was built in 1890 by H.B. Ball as a fanciful, brick Tudor-revival apartment house at the corner of Memorial Drive and Massachusetts Avenue, just west of the present MIT campus. Today, the elegant apartment house is known as Ashdown Court and is used as a residence for MIT graduate students.

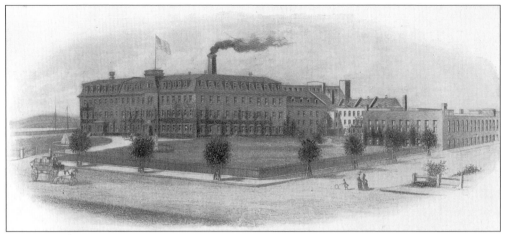

The Riverside Press was founded in 1852 by A.F. Lemon and Charles P. Clark. The press, located in a sprawling plant, was operated by Houghton, Mifflin & Company. It continued the tradition of book printing that was established in Cambridge in 1638 by Stephen Daye. Daye was the indentured servant of Mistress Glover, who set up a printing press to spread the Puritan belief—as all books had a religious implication. This press was the only one in the colony until 1674 when John Foster set up a press in Boston at the Sign of the Dove.

The Athenaeum Press was located in this elegant brick and brownstone lintel building in Cambridgeport. The building, designed by Lockwood, Greene & Company, was built in 1895 and contains a life-sized statue of Athena Nike surmounting the frontal pediment. Here, Ginn & Company published textbooks, which were distributed throughout the United States. Today, the restored building houses a number of professional offices.

Nine
BUSINESS AND INDUSTRY

The John C. Dow & Company opened in Cambridge in 1866. The factory produced fertilizers, soaps, and poultry supplies. Its specialty was Dow's Nitrogenous Superphosphate and Ground Bone Fertilizer. Notice the unusual canvas tents over the drivers of the delivery wagons—obviously a hot summer day when this photograph was taken in the late 1800s.

The New York Biscuit Company was best known for its Kennedy's Champion Biscuit, sold and enjoyed throughout the country. Established by Artemus Kennedy in 1839, the company made crackers and cookies by hand and delivered them locally in a "gaudy red van with pictures of Mr. Kennedy's two pretty daughters painted on the side." By 1890, the company had branches in every major city and a capital stock of $9 million. The Cambridgeport factory employed 650 hands and had a capacity of consuming from 300 to 400 barrels of flour per day in the production of crackers and biscuits.

The factory of the Mason & Hamlin Company was a large complex in Cambridgeport. The company was founded in 1854 by Henry Mason and Emmons Hamlin for the production of melodeons. It produced its first pianos in 1881 and shipped them to the salesroom at 146 Boylston Street, Boston, an area known as Piano Row. At the end of the 1800s, the Cambridgeport plant employed 400 people.

124

The Revere Sugar Refinery was established in 1871 on Miller's River in East Cambridge. The company refined sugarcane imported from the West Indies, producing both brown and white sugar. At the end of the 1800s, the six-story factory employed 130 people and produced 1,400 barrels of sugar per day. Here, teams are being loaded with barrels of refined sugar at the loading dock near the tracks of the Boston and Lowell Railroad.

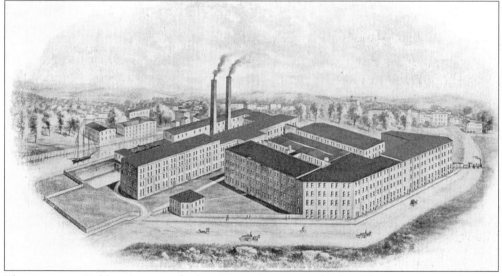

The American Rubber Company had its factory in East Cambridge. The company was founded in 1872 by R.D. Evans for the purpose of manufacturing boots, shoes, clothing, and wringer rolls. By the end of the 1800s, the company had 100 employees and 2 acres of floor space, which gave it the capacity to produce of 25,000 pairs of boots and shoes and 2,000 rubber coats and mackintoshes per day.

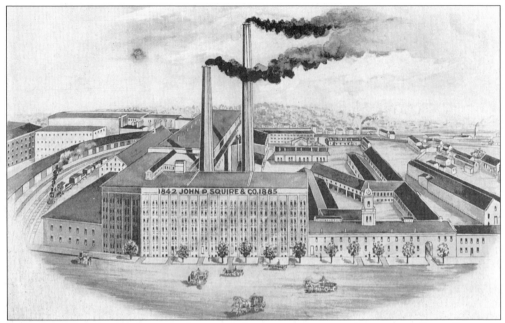

John P. Squire & Company had its slaughtering and curing factory on Gore Street in Cambridge, on the Somerville line. The Rev. Samuel A. Eliot once said that the company "reduced the packing of pork products to something resembling a fine art." At the end of the 1800s, the factory had 1,000 employees and a capacity of slaughtering 5,000 hogs a day.

John P. Squire started his career in 1838 as a clerk in the meat stall of Nathan Robbins in Fanueil Hall Market. By 1885, John P. Squire & Company in Cambridge was so prolific that the "magnitude of the business may be suggested by the statement that over 800,000 hogs are slaughtered annually at his factory."

The boiler works of William Campbell & Company was located on Sixth Street near Broadway in Cambridgeport. Established in 1873, the company built steel and iron steam boilers, rendering tanks, and jacket kettles. At the end of the 1800s, it had 30 employees.

The Coleman Brothers' Coal Wharf and Elevator was located on First Street in East Cambridge. The coal barge *Adelia Carelton* is discharging coal onto the elevator, where it will be stored until delivered throughout the area for heating and cooking uses.

At the end of the 1800s, Magazine Beach, once referred to as Captain's Island, attracted not only bathers but also well-dressed people who promenaded along the sand and watched those hearty enough to swim to the floating barge in the distance.

Acknowledgments

I would like to thank the following for their assistance in researching this book on Cambridge, Massachusetts. In many instances, these individuals have loaned photographs, stereoviews, and books on the history and development of the town, and I appreciate their continued support and interest: Charles Bahne; Anthony Bognanno; the Boston Athenaeu;, the Boston Public Library; Paul and Helen Graham Buchanan; the Cambridge Health Alliance; the Cambridge Historical Commission; the Cambridge Public Library; Frank Cheney; Elise Ciregna and Stephen Lo Piccolo; Edie Clifford; Regina K. Clifton; the Rev. Elizabeth Curtiss; Rupert A. M. Davis; the Honorable Francis H. Dewhay, mayor of Cambridge; Dexter; Edward W. Gordon; Helen Hannon; Janet Heywood, Friends of Mount Auburn Cemetery; Victor Jannette; Dan Kasuba; James Z. Kyprianos; Chris Mathias; the Milton Historical Society; Susan W. Paine; the Rev. Michael Parise; Jeannette Lithgow Peverley; Roger S. Pierce; Michael Price; Anthony and Mary Mitchell Sammarco; the late Charlotte Tuttle Clapp Sammarco; Rosemary Sammarco; Sylvia Sandeen; Robert Bayard Severy; Barbara Worthington Stebbins; John Sullivan; Amy Sutton, my editor; Anne and George Thompson; Kenneth Turino; William Varrell; the Victorian Society; New England Chapter; and Dorothy C. Wallace.